THE SUPREME COURT
A guide for bears

Isobel Williams

Foreword by Lord Neuberger

For Neil

Published in the United Kingdom by Isobel Williams, www.isobelwilliams.org.uk

First printed June 2017

Design: Dick Makin Imaging www.dmimaging.co.uk

ISBN 978-1-9997146-2-8

For information about the UK Supreme Court, please see www.supremecourt.uk

Acknowledgement
The author would like to thank the Justices, staff and bears at the Supreme Court of the United Kingdom and the Judicial Committee of the Privy Council for making every visitor feel welcome.

THE SUPREME COURT
A guide for bears

Foreword

The bears who are about to guide you around the Supreme Court are not only very charming creatures; they are also very popular.

Since the Court opened in 2009, around 2000 members of the bear family have left the Court for new loving homes around the UK and beyond.

We've even spotted some VIP foreign visitors quietly, even surreptitiously, make their way to our gift shop to 'adopt' a bear to take home with them.

It's good to know that the bears are travelling around the world, spreading the word about the UK's top appeal court as they go.

And in this book you are about to see them explain a bit about what our Court does (and doesn't do). Isobel Williams's drawings capture the essence of these inquisitive and endearing characters – and her words help bring to life some of the things they get up to when the Justices and staff aren't looking.

If you haven't yet had a chance, I hope that one day soon you will be able to visit the UK Supreme Court in the centre of London. We promise you a warm welcome, whether or not any cases are being heard at the time – and who knows, you might even spot one of our furry friends!

David Neuberger
President of the UK Supreme Court
June 2017

The Supreme Court on Parliament Square welcomes visitors. It's free, you don't have to book, and the souvenirs on sale downstairs in the café look just like you and me.

The Supreme Court building is home to many animals and heraldic beasts.

Words from the vow sworn by judges are etched on the inner glass doors.

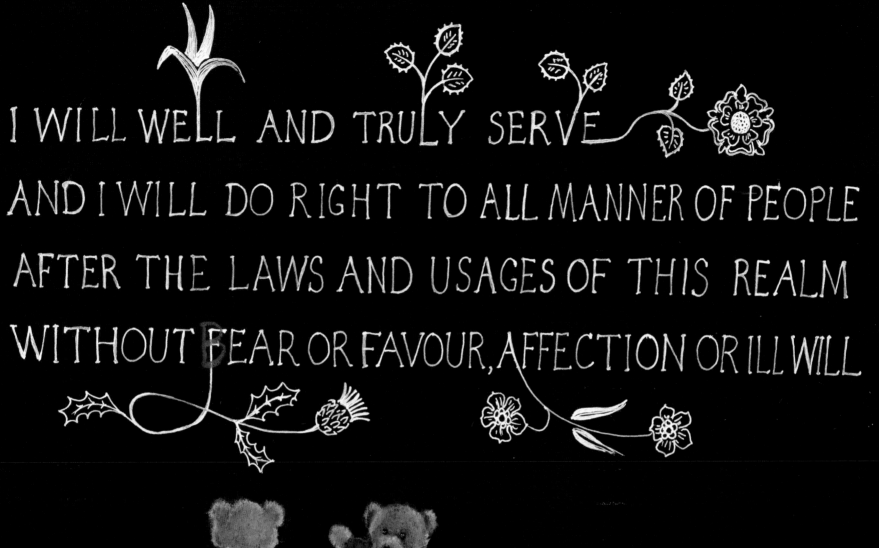

I WILL WELL AND TRULY SERVE
AND I WILL DO RIGHT TO ALL MANNER OF PEOPLE
AFTER THE LAWS AND USAGES OF THIS REALM
WITHOUT FEAR OR FAVOUR, AFFECTION OR ILL WILL

The Supreme Court is the highest court in the land. It hears appeals against judgments which have been made in other courts.

Barristers present legal arguments in front of five, seven or – if the issue is very serious – nine Justices.

The Supreme Court examines points of law. It does not rule on guilt or innocence.

This carved wooden bear is in Court 1

In the lower ground floor café
there is a bust of King Edward VII.

There is no gavel in the
British justice system.

During hearings, no photography
is allowed.

We are not in America.

In the Supreme Court there are no
witnesses, no cross-examination
and no jury.

It is only in some of the lower
courts that you may be tried
before…

...a jury of your bears.

The Supreme Court building used to be called Middlesex Guildhall.

Opened in 1913, it housed Middlesex County Council and Quarter Sessions (law courts), complete with prison cells.

After renovation, it re-opened in 2009 as the Supreme Court.

Everyone is welcome to observe Supreme Court hearings from the public seats, for just a few minutes or for a whole day.

This carved stone bear is in Court 3

The Judicial Committee of the Privy Council sits in the same building.

Its records date from 1386, when it was called the King's Council. The King was Richard II.

It is the highest court of appeal for many current and former Commonwealth countries, UK overseas territories, crown dependencies, military sovereign base areas and some ancient and ecclesiastical courts.

The Supreme Court contains the Middlesex Art Collection.

This painting of the Earl of Northumberland by Sir Joshua Reynolds is in Court 3, where the Judicial Committee of the Privy Council usually sits.

The earl became Lord Lieutenant of Middlesex, a member of the Privy Council and the 1st Duke of Northumberland.

He is buried across the road from the Supreme Court, in Westminster Abbey.

This portrait of Arthur Wellesley, 2nd Duke of Wellington (son of the Iron Duke who defeated Napoleon) hangs in Court 1.

He was Lord Lieutenant of Middlesex, a member of the Privy Council, Knight of the Garter and Master of the Horse.

His widow died in Surrey at Bearhill Park.

SIR JOHN FIELDING, Knt.

In Court 1 there is a portrait of Sir John Fielding.

Despite being blinded by botched surgery when he was 19, he ran a successful business and became the most innovative magistrate of his time, tackling highwaymen and street robbers.

With his half-brother, the writer and magistrate Henry Fielding, he invented the role of the detective by hiring thief-takers to investigate crimes; they became known as the Bow Street Runners. He also founded charities to rescue destitute children and helped to enforce laws on animal welfare. Controversially, he allowed court cases to be reported in the press.

His house in Bow Street wasn't big enough for all the court's business, so suspects were held in the pub over the road.

Today it is called the Globe, but then it was known as the Brown Bear.

There are Supreme
Courts in many other
countries, including the USA.

'The Constitution would not have
been noticeably affected if Sherman
Minton's chair had been occupied by a
stuffed teddy bear from 1949 to 1953.'
— *The History of the Supreme Court of
the United States*, vol. 12, William M.
Wiecek, CUP, 2006

The Supreme Court receives gifts from many countries. The display changes now and then; if you don't see the ones shown here you'll find plenty of others.

This bronze horse, poised on a swallow in flight, is a present from the Supreme People's Court of the People's Republic of China.

The marble polar bears, beneath a glass table top, are a gift from the Chief Justice of Canada.

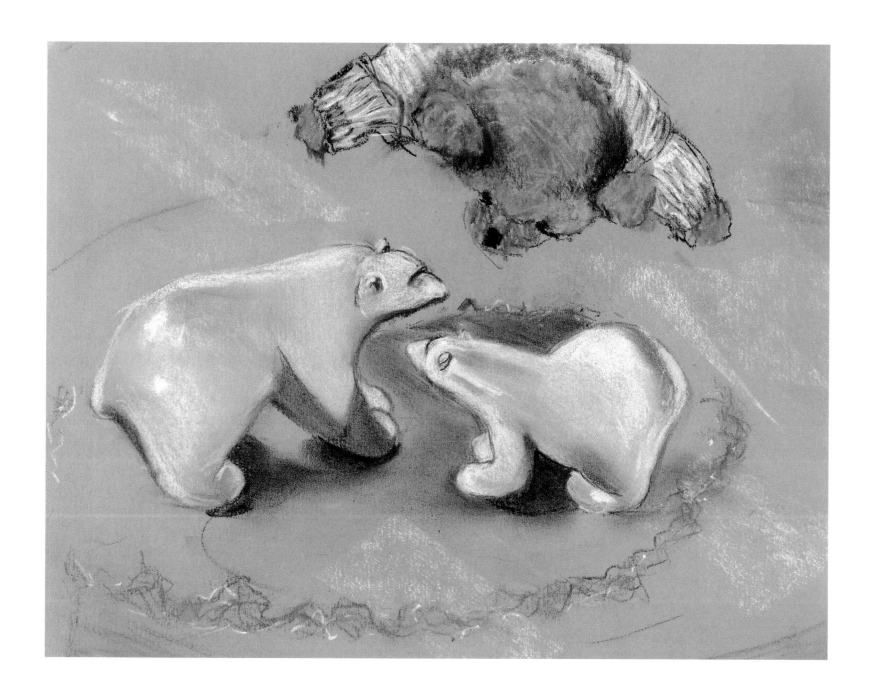

The Supreme Court carpet is designed by Sir Peter Blake, whose works include iconic record sleeves.

It contains national symbols: the thistle for Scotland, the flax flower for Northern Ireland, the Tudor rose for England and the leek for Wales.

A peacock, a boar, a bay horse, pelicans and a bear are in the arms of the Duke of Newcastle who was Prime Minister 1754–56. You will find them in a stained glass window on the main staircase of the Supreme Court.

The Latin motto VICIT AMOR PATRIAE means 'love of his country overcame [him]'. You could say 'patriotism conquers all'.

It hints at a line from Virgil's Aeneid: Vincet amor patriae laudumque immensa cupido ('Love of his country and a huge thirst for glory will prevail').

A quotation from the American First Lady and human rights campaigner Eleanor Roosevelt is etched into the glass screen of Court 2. Sometimes things that you write have unintended consequences.

Teddy bears are named after her uncle, Theodore Roosevelt, President of the United States from 1901 to 1909.

Barristers do not have to wear wigs or robes in the Supreme Court; most of them choose not to. The Justices do not wear robes except on ceremonial occasions.

The only person who always wears a gown is the Court Usher.

Bears are under-represented among the senior judiciary. But we believe we can sort that out for ourselves.

A poem, written by Sir Andrew Motion when he was Poet Laureate, is carved into two stone benches outside the building.

A THOUSAND BEARS OF JUDGMENT STRETCH BEHIN
WITH FAIRNESS AND WITH DUTY TO THE WORLD

NEW STRUCTURES BUT AN OLD FOUNDATION S
FOUR NATIONS SEPARATE BUT LINKED AS O

Not all bears are lucky enough to occupy a court.

If you would like to support bears (known to science as *Ursidae*), please look for a reputable charity which helps us, and avoid products or entertainments which exploit us. Thank you.